A SENSE OF NORTH

DAVID UNDERDOWN

Cinnamon Press
:: small miracles from distinctive voices ::

Published by Cinnamon Press
Meirion House
Tanygrisiau
Blaenau Ffestiniog
Gwynedd, LL41 3SU
www.cinnamonpress.com

The right of David Underdown to be identified as author of this work has been asserted by him in accordance with the Copyright, Designs and Patent Act, 1988. Copyright © 2019 David Underdown.
ISBN: 978-1-78864-045-9

British Library Cataloguing in Publication Data. A CIP record for this book can be obtained from the British Library.

Designed and typeset in Palatino by Cinnamon Press. Printed in Poland.

Cover design by Adam Craig.

Cinnamon Press is represented in the UK by Inpress Ltd and in Wales by the Welsh Books Council.

Acknowledgements

Some of these poems (or early versions) have appeared in *The North*, *Envoi* and *Bracken*, in anthologies published by Live Canon, New Writing Scotland, Norwich Writers' Circle and the Wenlock Poetry Festival. I am also grateful to David Constantine, Maura Dooley and Cicely Gill for their wise advice and encouragement.

Contents

for Claire

A Sense of North

The secret of flying

The breakthrough is to stop thinking
about aerodynamics. Concentrate
on the immeasurable pleasures
of floating above roofs
and the open mouths of chimney pots

stems of road budding
houses, the rumple of fields
and, beyond, the dark spot of a copse
or how the river feels
up into its tree-lined tributaries.

And later, after that first step

                                into space
the art of soaring on thermals
of passing over boundaries
a sense of north.

Cabin doors to automatic

Always that slow start to parting
after the fine days
silences forming like smirr

frayed ends of thoughts
where nothing holds fast when we embrace
you have already slipped away

and a change in the pitch of the ventilation
the real moment of leaving
the shift of pressure in my ears

cabin doors to automatic
seals slipping into place
now your air is different from mine

beyond the glass
shrouded buildings moving
a glimpse of angled trees

and at ten thousand feet
still a world that hangs together
with crosshatched streets and the line of a river

held in place by gravity that I've escaped
but even now is bearing down
there where we were

as past the wings come speeding shoals of cloud
and I burst into light
and empty sky.

Poem

I've started to wonder
how it must feel

to live in your skin.
For years we have shared

a bed, our breakfasts,
births, and deaths,

like the east and west bank
of the same river,

but when you tell me
your back aches again

or you need a cup of tea
I cannot tell

whether your ache, your need,
is just like mine or something else.

And today a jade-green moth
paused on our window's sill.

You called for me to see
but it had gone.

Morning tea

Waking a little before you
I go downstairs to make tea
as I have for thirty years
in the dark if it's still winter
and always the same two mugs
the kitchen at rest before the day
one scoop in the pot, milk
and wait to let it brew.

Back upstairs we sit in bed
in the dark if it's still winter
to sip our morning tea
and ask each other how we've slept
and talk about the day
each day in the same way
as if there'd never been another way,
as if it could always be like this.

My favourite shirt

After all this time my favourite shirt
the one I never have to think about
or wonder if it's right, has gone,
worn out, a tear across its back
where countless times I've tucked it in.
And now I look more closely
the collar's frayed. Cuffs too.
In places it's so thin it is diaphanous.
When did this occur? When
was the first time someone might have looked
and idly thought: 'Bit shabby'?

I wonder how it is that we lose grace.
It does not happen suddenly
though that is how you notice it,
the thinning of the lips, the brightness gone
from this person who remains your friend.

Against the tide

Down here the river has widened,
already flooding salt for half the day,
mud-bound for the rest.
The tides wipe clean
the mazy prints of wading birds.
Below the bridge there's broken masonry,
the pier where the cobbles stop,
and then it's willow herb and buddleia
all the way to the sea's flat-line.

Easy to see why you linger
to watch the gulls circle,
catching the hum from the bypass.
If you could, you would turn
and find your way upstream again
past viaducts and fat meadows,
solid farmsteads set round by trees,
and feel, as the land draws in,
the younger waters quicken.

There, where the uplands open out
you would track each beck
up to its marshy watershed
to understand how it started,
the long journey to the sea
and what alternatives there nearly were.
But the tide is turning,
colder wind roughening the water,
staining it dark, draining it out.

The lugworm fails to foresee
the beak of the curlew

sensing as the sea falls away
while not knowing anything for how could you
without a brain or slightest recall
of how twice each day the water ebbs
(silt settling under its own weight)
then rises on the tide's tug
to swither over where to turn
but never, notwithstanding, knowing
that it has re-turned, is no longer gone,
and all the time designed with a need
to wind and burrow, to worm a way,
to force a passage grain by grain
so that, within each segment,
ooze that was without becomes embodied,
the filtered substance you inhabit
becoming part of you in turn...
and the quaking up there
having no meaning whatsoever
until it is repeated, frantic
for that last instant
of what they call
light.

Song for the lock keeper on the Carlisle to Solway Canal c. 1853

Here, where fresh mingles with salt,
they say the tide sweeps in faster than horses.
Gulls gather among the shoals,
stand along the braided courses
of sand and river. They keen, cries caught
in cold, thin air; their circling
leaves no room for thought
or knowing on what they are waiting.

But listen, now they have found food, something
already dead, something no good has come to,
and I, keeper of water, guardian of levels, sing
of joining-up, of high and low,
of how all was once within my care.
I watch for trapped stars, stare
into the bucket of clouded sky, count
the tides that ride beneath the unseen moon.

There is no peace in this place. See—
it nags and frets and skirls.
What was set in stone is becoming what will be,
settling piece by piece,
one part into another, all worn down
until high places lie low, hollows
silt up, all deeds are undone
in the meeting of land and river and sea.

Lock work

Here is where I saw him,
not a man, more a creature from somewhere else,
head as round as the moon, and copper,
limbs encased in rubber, pillared legs,
each booted foot weighed down by lead.

The lock gates spilled soup-brown water
as he sank, the pipe from his head flexing,
the pump coughing to keep him going.
My last glimpse: through the window in his head,
his watchful eyes.

The woman on a bicycle

Here she comes Halloo! Halloo!
With a ding of her bell
And her hat askew
Like the picture I drew.

Round the wheels rush.
I cannot see their spokes
But in my head I've heard
A hush of shouting words.

Look! High above it all
Like the raven in my book
She's speeding with her news.
She's riding for a fall.

*

Not just her tallness, the man-high woman
with her hat as black as a mass;
not just her shouting
like a workman or a footballer;
or the basket of books in the bicycle's prow
ploughing a mad furrow
along the silence of the street;
but all these things together
and moving at speed.

*

Only much later
I saw her strangeness
on that bike, how she might be
in torment, like a fight, but just her,
and moving at speed
down the familiar road.

And was it only me
or did no one say a thing?
As if it was normal, all those words
in a shouting voice
and in black
and going so fast.

Springboard

He is on his own now, up there
where everyone's watching
and weighing his chances

but only she knows the three breaths
he takes before the short leap out,
before the twist and double somersault.

He will enter the water as a needle
punctures skin. And disappear.
She takes the breaths with him, her first born.

She takes the breaths with him,
sees him somersault
and disappear.

The measuring stick

Yesterday I found it in the shed:
plain deal, six foot of two by two
planed to an even softwood grain.
It used to stand beside the bedroom door.

Against a hard-back, levelled scalp to pole,
each head would crane the extra quarter inch
vying for indelible proof
as marks were made and set aside,
then re-consulted on the next significant date.

The biroed lines in blue and black
had almost slipped away. I marked them in,
each mark for a particular day.

Out of sight

Not on the train but at Central afterwards:
you were halfway down the platform
when I glimpsed your back, thinner now,
shoulders no longer really broad enough
to wear an overcoat, a step
that hardly kept pace with the crowd.
But that same classy leather bag.

And I nearly thought to catch you up
and say, but by then you were through
the barrier and out of sight.

Tipping point

For two weeks time has lost its limits
as if we're compassless
and out of sight of land.
We've been winging our days
without thinking how they reckon up.
Then, last night, the talk about the taxi
and something tipped.
                              I am wondering
about the children, what the garden's doing
how it will be to sleep in our own bed.
Like when your brother said
after the doctor: that sudden glimpse
of just how little time is left.

Compass

It could have been just one more of those
strange-but-true stories: nine thousand miles,
the long circle painted across continents
and all those generations, each
discovering its particular part
in the journey, the right place to lay eggs;

but then, clearing the shed,
that one gram miracle on the ledge
its still bright wings lodged against the pane
the body's furred shell dried out
with somewhere in the earth outside
a chrysalis ready for warmer days

and you, tucked in your crib up there,
no map and only your heart's compass.

Charlotte Brontë's boots

Your choosing them: what took your fancy
must have been the compact chiseled toes
capped by black leather, soft
as human skin might be.

No Vibram, no Goretex, no inner sole.
You could never walk roughshod in these
over your reverend father, over Branwell,
over your dead sisters,

yet here they are, left and right,
under glass now. In fine or inclement weather
each morning you would lace them tight
to go about the business of your day.

More here than fabric and the skin of animals.
The same fingers held these as held the pen
in that room upstairs, the one where Jane
and Bessie Lee and Rochester were born.

Brown, patterned like Laura Ashley
and tiny, more like gloves than boots,
they must have encased your feet,
your boniness, white beneath your stockings.

Who warmed them, those feet of yours,
sore and cold from moors and rough cobbles?
Who would you trust to feel the space
between each toe, or hold that instep in their hand?

Exhibits from the Surgeons' Hall

The mummified head c.1200 B.C.

Someone so treasured
that when the time came
men laboured on her body
with unguents and clever implements
to furnish all she would need.

Bathed and wept over
she is dry now, like an old gourd.
Where her tongue was loose
and filled the mouth of her lover
her lips purse for a barren kiss.

The foetal skeletons c.1870

In order to instruct students
he has constructed a tableau
of tiny skeletons

their individual bones
hung in a halted dance
the tallest at the rear

and sizing down an arc of eight,
no, nine small fellows
following their smallest leader

specimens from still births
or torn from their womb
in a panic of blood.

In the tranquillity
of his laboratory
he rendered out their bones

and re-assembled them
a band of small people
who never became what they were.

The foot c.1916

Left, size 8 or 9,
narrow fit, high arched
with nails as trim as cockles
and graceful until you see
how gangrene caught hold
and flesh mottled to rotten brawn:
where the surgeon's saw found purchase
a soft moon of bone, and round it
a flowering like torn fungus
through which frayed nerve ends
carried signals of flex and stretch
and the dull ache of marching.

Heavenfield

Walking the Wall—Segedunum, Vindolanda,
Aesica—the mile-castles strung out
like beads across Britannia's neck
to choke out Scots and Caledones.
Grey light highlights northern wastes
while southwards the sun shimmers over fat lands
struck through by old, straight roads.

It didn't work of course. There's no knowing
how empires give up, only that they will.
Something changes and they are stricken
by canker or wilt, root-bound—
Vercovicium turns to Housesteads,
tight packed barrack blocks just floor plans.
Then, from fallen stonework, Haltwhistle crops up.

Masons have a field day, the border dissolved,
but always building, building to be done.
And this wet summer I've found myself
washed up here, wading in the slurry of history:
belligerent tribes, St Oswald, reivers' raids
and there in the mud an altar for auxiliaries to offer thanks,
and here a battleground called Heavenfield.

Benediction

Someone up here
has felt the need to offer thanks

and seeing where a spring flows
straight from the rock

has made a blade
of rhododendron wood

to turn as water falls
and through a spindle

drive a drum of bronze
that reels out blessings.

Snows melt.
Water flows

and as the wheel spins it sings
and round the empty valley

for any passing living thing
there rise what may be prayers.

Notes for a letter to my son

Now you are old enough to know
not always to do as you're told
here is some advice.

*

Standing on Dover Beach what should we do,
whose special oddity
is knowing that we're here?

Regarding the rough and the smooth
mostly I'd opt for the rough, that remains
lodged in the brain long after easy times have gone.

*

Life is not a bowl of cherries.
It is not a rehearsal. Or a gift.
Life is not fair. It was never meant to be   fair.

Life is for living.
It's a doddle, a bed
of roses, of nettles, of nails.

*

The psalmist said 'my cup runneth over'
meaning that, on a humdrum day,
he'd glimpsed a particle of god

for nothing is significant
unless we make it so: all there is
is what we find ourselves.

*

Whether you'd want a dog's life
depends on the breed: Labradors are fine,
and Welsh Collies provided there are sheep around.

*

The life of Riley offers a supply of Guinness.
The meaning of life is not the holy grail
or the life of Brian.

Aristotle's good life was *eudaimonia*
which sounds like a disease
but means the good that comes from flourishing.

*

So how will you choose:
to be admired, or loved?
To be amazed, or feared?

*

Name your blessings—not as comforts
or contentments but as rents in the curtain
that let through light

or remembering how sun can seep
past the edge of things
to make a halo round the ordinary.

*

To be ambushed by joy, that's the point,
a glint of treasure
lingering as an after-burn.

Facts of life

We went walking, father and son,
and you chose the long way back
to give time for all you wanted to say.
And I, an unwilling listener,
sensed only how it troubled you

though never afterwards in all those years
did we speak of it again, not once.
For why did you need to put it into words
when through those days of living in that house
I'd watched you and her live your lives
together, their tight wholeness
and the loose frayings that would never be mended?

Home brew

Father's wine had its own lexicon
of awfulness: mousy, ropy, goaty…
his proud but uncontested claim:
you can make wine from anything.
And to prove it would hoard unwanted produce:
parsnips, pears, beetroot, marrows, peas,
crabs and sloes from the hedgerows,
and douse them in a filthy bucket
with boiling water laced with sugar
to let the errant air-borne yeasts
that hung about the nether regions of our house
perform their alchemy.

And yet to go with Sunday roast
he'd find a dusty bottleful
of pink, sparkling fruitfulness
that made us chatter and laugh, and once
made mother throw her empty glass
over her shoulder as if she didn't care.

Happy hour

Again, from somewhere,
the amber idea
has
    sidled
        up
filled waiting mindspace,
blunted this morning's curiosity.

Once conceived the notion nags,
weaves tendrils through all other thoughts
crouched
      down
        there
tight as a balled root,
fixed as a fat tick.

Need fidgets
like too much change in a trouser pocket:
its restless
      breathless
        presence
strung taut across the mind's wires
grows gimlet sharp.

But, at the bar at last,
for five full minutes or maybe more
it's pure magic
      celestial bliss
        supernal blessing
optimism in a straight-sided glass
stillness settling like dew on parched grass.

The Dodgem Man

Six years old, with parents argued into line
and pockets full of pocket-money change
I'm off up that peculiar street again
where at its end the square is extra-bright
with mirrored light and loud with hurdy-gurdy.
Waltzing roundabouts come spinning to a halt

and there he is, The Dodgem Man,
high on the smell of static from his sparking cars,
the jingle of his leather bag of change.
Within my head the music drains away
and crouched behind the wheel
I lunge and swerve
to glance past others right and left,
bumped and bumping,
jolted back by cars that jar
then pirouette and shimmy off
with me, beyond control, in hot pursuit…
until the power is cut.   Stranded
I make my shaky way to steadier ground

and he's still there.
I fumble round for more,
turn pockets inside out to find his half a crown
and ever since have done the same
to buy just one more ride.

Pulling out

That time out in the outside lane
as in a fog a decision made
not in the brain but in a hunch
of shoulders a clench of wheel
a leaning forward to get past sooner.
That moment again for such crazy odds
so slight a gain gleaned for such monstrous outlay
and the stretch of road ahead so short and shortening
clear yes but with the bend so near
eyes locked on all its possibilities
breath held foot waiting for the evidence
that foot-to-floor will change anything
start the slow motion edge past
to where brakes can't help
because the time's too near now
too up against it
the gleam of silver rounding
the bend ahead
making the stakes real
though this time pulling through
to inside space that's opened up
to veer back, slump back
as if this was all one more trivial thing.

Goldcrest on auto-pilot

It was one of those spring-loaded mornings
when even the news is cheerful, and me,
top of the food chain, with shiny teeth
and we wouldn't have normally met but we did
on this wide-open Tuesday we two were to share:

the one, just passing with a tune in my head;
the other, kamikaze by the conservatory,
the nation's smallest bird
decked out, in flash feathers
and golden fascinator.

Already two months into winter
and if you had been human
you'd have thought you were doing well
with the longer days not that far off;
but you didn't because your one gram brain

knew only the intricacies of flight,
the link between a black-bead eye and pin tack beak
and the barbed curl of your claws on the branch
that you thought you'd clocked in the window's glass
the instant you hit.

In this wood

But in this wood, he said, the end of many of the trees
has come sooner than you might have thought
whether through storms, winds catching at their branches
in sudden gusts leaving them uprooted, their limbs
thrust out as if to keep their balance as they fell,
or through lightning strikes, trunks riven and charred
and even the inside stretched like torn ligament,
their sinews blackened by fire, or some toppled,
their neighbours falling and upending them,
and though many still survive some die simply
after the passage of their years, and strangely, he said,
even after the dying off of leaves and drying out of roots
the fallen ones live another sort of life
accommodating creatures, and fungi that blossom on their boughs
or mycelium that consumes the dying xylem cell by cell
so that timber once as hard as oak or dense as beech
becomes no more solid than cork, say, or balsa,
crumbly when pressed, or finally just dust
heaped around remains of their great trunks
or in many cases the doomed wood is burrowed through
by beetles seeking shelter in its hidden interior,
a home and food for offspring when they hatch.

Hens roosting

As light begins to fade
from wherever they have wandered
they begin a gradual return
heads cocked to scratch and peck.

Soon the first enters the coop
her feet scraping the bare planks
the small commotion of wings
her settling down along the beam

as one and then another follow
to take a place among the shifting feet
wing to wing with no idea of what might be feared
in the half-darkness that will become full-darkness.

Always one is loath to hurry
descending the muddy bank to stand
head cocked and sensing old forest ways
of roosting high among the branches.

And once returning late to latch the door
the coop empty and looking up
boughs festooned as if with presents
the stir of feathers beneath the open sky.

Thrift

Because having less now, there will be more
tomorrow, or in matters such as the importance
of bottle tops, bus fares, the re-employment
of wrapping paper and lengths of string,

or because of the rightness
of make-do-and-mend
when it comes to construction
of a fence say, or a hen coop;

how my father carved
misshapen chunks of apple
between where maggots hid
or a bruise had spread;

and how distinct it is from meanness
taking no account of wealth,
but where, on seaside ledges, its pink flowers thrive,
needing so little to prove its steadfastness.

A man would call them his collection…

but these, assembled with no guiding hand, have gathered
slowly, around your presence in this house:

lustres of sea-green glass, spangled poppies tapering to a spout,
a wave of Wedgwood blue where dragons lurk below an undulating rim.

And best, the one I'm holding now, its tender feelers reaching out,
ultramarine shot through by bolts of misted green —

like stems through steamed-up glass. Slender in the hollow of my palm,
it nestles, just where your fingertip might trace a figure eight

and waits, with no demands, an easy, generous pourer,
to be brimful of milk and offer itself up.

Birthday poem

So many more to look back on now:
they merge like the curling crocodile
of chancy dominoes we used to stand
tile against tile until we'd used them all.

The game was always to find more
and yet a single slip, a misplaced fingertip,
and one would start to topple, then the next
along the line until the very end.

Fountain

Yesterday returneth not.
Tomorrow perchance cometh not.
Today is thine, misuse it not.
                    (Inscription at Formakin House, Renfrewshire, Scotland)

Back then, where dead leaves lie in drifts,
fish nosed, golden between dark stems of lilies.
Within the courtyard's stone embrace
she watched them swim through her reflection,
and dreamed of babies.

*

She has been told by Mrs Patterson
that the eggs are already inside her
lined up like bottles waiting to be filled.
And only a few, or maybe none,
will ever know who they are.

*

Through the arch again and in almost no time,
beneath the audience of broken windows,
they are running races, round and around;
and collapse breathless, laughter overflowing
just where she was then.

Birth day

When the raw air burned in your chest—
slap-slap, you choked on its coldness.

Then swaddling, and water
as warm as that nest of blood,
the slither and thither of hands,
high sounds and low sounds.

What you missed?
It was her strong heart,
a message not in a bottle
but from outer space.

The race of your own blood
through its failing heart
was when your voyage ended.
Then cold silence.

No time for partings.

In the park

Six weeks old
and suddenly I'm someone again.
Heads turn. A woman half my age
has stopped to talk.

I hold you close
to feel you grow
a heart's beat away
as warm as my blood:

your head on my shoulder
is building your world;
splayed feet
hopscotch air.

In heavy summer heat,
the scent of spring you bring
trips pheromones
in each unwary passer-by.

First steps

The shift from hands and knees
to almost vertical
is just another experiment

a weightlifter's stretch—
cautious, torso tense,
arms wide, legs flexed—

                             leading to the unplanned start
       two steps
halt (unscheduled) to check stability
      feet planted not so firmly
                wide of the line of travel
                        elbows skew
     and off again in twos and threes
for this is definitely fun
     the destination still undetermined
             but at the moment approaching at a fair lick
and easy enough to look around
     for support and encouragement
          which turns out to be fatal
     prompting the last lurch
          the two more wobbly steps
and final collapse

into open arms.

Puppies

The men hold them in threes in wide-cupped hands
waiting for *gringos* to buy them and take them away.
The puppies are black and white and fawn, and one is chocolate.

Their noses are pink as fingertips.
Hoisted high above the sidewalk in the winter sun
they do not wonder why, for they are warm in the men's hands

and too sleepy to understand their lives could change.

The boy is waiting to see what will happen.
He is no more concerned than the puppies.
He feels the wrinkles of their foreheads

and how the paws are bigger than they ought to be.
But his favourite has a name
and when the *gringos* come he holds his breath.

Logan discovers time

Not quite two, he's in a dream.
The tick-tock never stops.
The hands are moving
but they do not move.
He is watching
the sound of passing time:
the polished wood,
the painted face,
and in the box
beneath the glass
its brassy beating heart.
Tick-tock it goes, tick-tock
through bedtime, breakfast,
playtime, tea.

Transfixed, he knows
it's called a clock but why,
behind the ticks, does silence grow?
He watches it, tick-tock,
clocks that it's there but not
that each tick-tock will come,
and go. Tick-tock.

Dandelion clock

At that time of year they would have been
on any roadside in England, at edges
of meadows or gardens, in cracks between slabs;
and your not-quite-two-year-old mind
with an unfilled shelf waiting
for what we noticed that afternoon
just where the alley to our house
widened to a bank of untended grass:
how, when only days before, everywhere
their yellow faces were so densely interleaved
and multiplied in upon themselves,
now they were opened out, puckered,
standing straight on milky stalks;
so there they were, the dandelion clocks,
in hundreds; and not just ready, poised
at that very instant of that afternoon
when we could dawdle past with time
to pluck one and for me to say
See these, do you know they tell the time?
and blow them off in hard puffs
their seeds drifting from their heads
in ones and twos and whole furry clusters
to catch the sun as it shone down that alleyway
on that afternoon, us holding the empty stems
like little baldies; and you, having no interest in,
no notion of time, saw not seeds
but what grown-ups call fairies
that drifted from our hands to settle
somewhere that could never be discovered.

Shadow lands

I've forgotten how to do the rabbit
but there, look, it's a spider, big
as my hand, and coming after you.

Only just two, you don't quite get it yet
but pat the wall splay-fingered
and where the hole in the sun
shrinks to your shape—*pat, pat*—it's there.

Years ago your mum and I
balanced one-legged on the beach
and from the monster's head
four arms waved back;

and better still that Boxing Day
when, though the sun went down mid-afternoon,
for five full minutes she and I
danced halfway down a purple cliff.

Now I'll have to learn the knack again,
may even remember to look up
to watch my own-shaped shadow
stride across the mountains' sides.

Dark star

I wish I could remember its name
that small, unremarkable town
down in the stifling South
near Avignon perhaps or Carcassonne—

and only for one night but so hot
that after confit and a whole bowl of cherries
we strolled the streets finger to finger in the dark
returning to the narrow alleyway
to fumble for keys but find the door open
worn wood opening easily
and feel our way up winding stairs
hand by hand on the walls
and at last the tiny room
lit by starlight and through an open window
over undulating roofs—

and when we lay drenched on coarse sheets
amongst discarded blankets, bolsters, clothes
waiting blindly for desire to gather
how that night was
how we imagined it might have been
and broken only by dawn and swallows
and still like the pull of a dark star.

Or any other safety

They are out there on the ice—
the sighted one and the blind—
hand in hand and blessed
with a gift of movement
to glide as if in spate
out on the edge.

And as I watch, look, she's let go
and he is free, trusting the space ahead
that is no longer dark but ablaze
with the glint of all the lost light
he feels streaming round his face.

What would you say, she said,
if I told you we were closer then
than ever in our lives
trusting our freedom with no need
for any place to be hidden
or any other safety?

That night I left you

That night I left you, as on the night before
and the night before that, spent
but still breathing. It was time to sleep.
Yet I knew the odds, didn't I, the risk I took?
And when the phone call came at two
it was no surprise to have to get dressed,
and drive the empty, orange-lit roads
back to the corridor, the room, the silent nurse.
Your final warmth had not yet quite dispersed.

And next time round you would have thought
I would have learned, after a whole day
of holding her hand, not to just pop out
for that breath of air while she was taking her last.
I could have played safe, not taken the chance—
and though I'm certain neither of you knew,
I know. And at the end I failed you.

Unstopped

Before sleep

During those last days
of lengthening shadows
a quiet sadness
after the long-awaited treat,
the trip of a lifetime.

The last visit but one

Not much of you left now
save slack skin, liver-spotted
by twentieth-century sun.

In your eyes still
anger, though more often fear

and today, for a moment
a small smile
at seeing your boy.

Talking to the dead

As if it was the breath you lost
unstopped my mouth how is it
now you've gone I can
say the truths between us?

What should I tell you
who for a while live on in me?
What discourse should we have
who know no more

than that for now at least
through these last open chinks
we hear each other speak?
What is it I should try to say?

What is it but love?
What is it, too late, but love?

Stories

I am keeping your stories.
They are safe with me for now
in the space where I still see
your face like a picture
preserved under glass.

They will dwell in my mind
for a while but fade
until I too am gone
and no one is there
to know who you were.

The whole man

Twelve years now
and there is a distance
so when I glimpse you

in your garden say,
smoke rising from a pile of leaves,
or by the river casting off,

it is the whole man I see
not just knotted hands
clutching your chair;

like the shape of land,
shadows gathering
but still a slant of sun.

Mrs Dalloway

After The Hours

She is caught in time, suspended
within this moment singled out
from the broad flow that brought her here.
Soon she will be swept downstream

but for now she is alone and knows
what it is like to have been conjured up
and find all this just once
as if by a trick of the light.

For this choosing of roses
she is judge and prisoner on parole.
It will be by yellow roses that she remembers
the empty room, the overflowing vase.

So well trailed, death when it comes
still shocks—the figure on the windowsill,
the sunshine spilling past to fill the room—
the easy shift, the toppling down,

the window occupied only by sky.

Tamil funeral

Your face with your name and your dates
are pasted on lampposts and fences
all the way to the place where you lived.

The bus and the rickshaw drivers
are waiting for minutes
that if you were here would be yours.

They have laid what was you
in its box by the side of the road
like a load that's too heavy to bear.

Between broken silences
your widow, your son, and the men
and the boys throwing firecrackers,

stand at your coffin
with all its shiny trimmings.
They are saying goodbye.

Although you left yesterday
they are saying goodbye
as if you have still not gone.

St Hilda's Priory

The place: unfurnished land
open to the wind and blessed
by wide skies and sea-light.

The burial ground: compact,
an estate of wooden crosses
timber-roofed to keep out rain.

The names: christian only,
no dates of coming
or passing. Agnes, Nancye, Mary-Nina.

The cats, in their own enclave.
Tabitha, Caedmon, Bluey,

and the men, skilful, of good standing,
tending chrysanthemums, salvia,
passion flowers, rhubarb.

Vows: taken long since,
before the three day week,
the miners' strike, Afghanistan.

Offices: observed each day—
Matins, Lauds, Prime—
followed to their end point.

The abbot's pond

The carp in the pond are plump. They lead nice lives
in water that is neither hot nor cold.

They skirt the reeds untroubled by boats or beaks.
No need to dart or flit—the abbot had the herons killed.

A monk arrives to scatter bread. The carp nudge up,
take it in a wet kiss, their mouths soft coral round a gaping maw.

They take what is offered.
Bread and fishes, a miracle.

*

It feels like any other day
the day they drain the pond:

the Abbot's men at the weir wrestling with the chains
the sluice gates easing in their grooves.

Water ebbs. Mud spreads.
Weed lies exhausted.

The men do not bother with nets. They have clubs
and leather bags, a cart with an open tub.

Shrine

The narrow path is steep
with scents of pine and juniper that lead you on
to where a lintel at the cavern's mouth
will make you stoop so low
as to leave the outer world behind.
Enter, and all falls away,
though you, a frail and used-up thing,
and hunched, are still in hope,
for once inside the roof is lofty, almost limitless.
From waves of ancient seas, stone lolls in tongues.
And there, within, no god, but a reminder
of what a god might be: a simple table,
faded cloth, gifts that some might misjudge poor,
small money, keepsakes, herbs as grateful prayers.

To be there for an hour, and still,
is more than some can stand, but do
and you'll leave naked in yourself
as if unclothed of need, and shuffle out
to blink in new-found light
with sun upon your head.

Herr Schmidt surprises the visitors

He has chosen the chancel
among the smell of small prayers
and the grainy bulk of stone.
Trunks of columns rise, recede
in fluted branches vaulting out
to interlace across the void.

And today, this man from Germany,
in baggy trousers and a dowdy jacket
as ordinary as Wednesday
among the random crowd of gawpers
launches a *basso profundo*
that fills the morning with ancient words.
Kyrie eleison, Lord have mercy.
We are peering from a window
we did not know was there.

A tentative history of words

The beginning of words was no more
than grunts or nuzzle-noises in the dark.
How then did they leap from dull original,
spilling out from their plain runnel
to bind brother to sister, neighbour
to neighbour, people into entire nations?
How did they colonise tables and houses,
swerve and veer, fail like fallen stars
yet sputter up in embers?

In half-light we whisper,
straining our ears for music,
the boots of a band on the cobbles,
pipes fading down the hill;
we mutter words in patterns
to set waves dancing through our arteries,
hiss steam in our still waters.

Pitter-patter thoughts,
half meant, half felt.
Black-on-white flurry of shapes.
They print off page by page.
Each end-stopped paragraph
that echoes afternoons, or months
of meanings gathered in
is hemmed round word by word.

And at the centre, hollowed out,
all that's been left unsaid, still there,
breathed wordlessly: caress, flinch,
a gradual filtering off, the faltering
intake of breath so real it's like fear.

Among the translators

We sat together in that airless hall
weaving justifications for what we do,
how we mould the words of one language
into words of another that are easy on the ear
for readers who seek instruction or amusement
each of us in a poor way striving merely to be of use,
and he allowing his head to fall while minutes lengthened
and his face to sink to a mask, let no hint slip of his intentions,
but of an instant bolted up and spoke, his eyes sharp and full of blaze
of how the people have been blinded by such hate of all who are foreign
and, turning in upon themselves against all who they feel do not belong
or who should no longer be their concern because there is no room,
hanker to blame them, as if this new-found misery is their fault,
and how it is the task of all who work with words never
to let their meaning slip or disallow their angularity
or carefulness and especially when words speak
of suffering or anger at the plight of others
or of fellows, or even of those they love,
it is needful to speak out what is true.
And as he spoke we all fell silent
and looking at each other knew.

Geography

People learn geography the hard way
discovering the meaning of countries
by crossing borders through barbed wire,
escaping barefoot to find out
about mountains, understanding deserts
through a whole summer of hunger
and the smell of carcasses.

Bolton, Bury, Rochdale, Oldham, Ashton:
fifty years on I can recite
the towns of the Cotton Crescent,
point to pink dominions across the globe
and reel off their states and capitals.
With a ruler I can pencil in
the band around the Earth where trade winds blow.

While cabin lights were dimmed,
I've watched where sun would rise
and seen the world to be a sphere in space;
looked down on icebergs strewn
like crumbs across a tablecloth; looked up
at the Twin Towers with no sense
of what might happen next.

If I sent a postcard to myself
from all the places where my body's been—
Wish you were here— and read them in my chair
I'd still not comprehend
the way to breathe in a locked truck,
or know the stench of people penned
in an open boat half way across the Med.

Notes for a solitary walk

For M.W. 1951 - 2014

This morning you are walking for her,
a small thing you can do, on a day
of deep green shadows and granite glitter,
that, if she were here, she would love.

Today, as she is not here,
you will not go the usual way
across the burns through stands of birch
where the dog would flex at the scent of deer,

but further, up the glen where even in her lifetime
the last men were still mining the hill.
You will shin up that shoulder of Cioch na' Oighe
to see the whole Clyde laid out,

just how, if she had ever had the chance,
she would have chosen to arrange it—
the named near hills and the unnamed hills of the horizons
and the spaces of water between.

You will walk south along your home's spine
for her to count its line of rocky vertebrae
and marvel at the openness
of all these lands of the West.

You will talk to her of travelled roads
and also of oceans you might have crossed
if there had been time, until,
reaching the lip of Coire Lan,

you will leave the broad path and drop down
below Am Binnein to the White Water
that leads (with no time now to stop)
past home to the indifferent sea.

The psychology of paths

The selection of paths

Think first whether you really need one
or if, rather than rely on others,
you might make your own.
Be suspicious of any too broad or even-surfaced
or any leading straight to somewhere popular.
Way-marks are easily missed, signposts reversible,
yet a circular path is fit only for amateurs.
Always choose a path by its cover:
moss is a good sign
or the spoor of rare animals.

The terminology of paths

A tunnel is not a path; a rainbow is not a path;
a corridor is not a path, even in your mind;
lanes are not paths save those with grassy centres.
Flight-paths designed by pigeons or prescribed
for jumbos need specialist skills.
A staccato path results in stepping-stones.
The path of the wind can lead to dunes
requiring major detours.
Rights of way are a reason for scepticism;
paths for the blind may be invisible;
a secret path leads to the spot marked X.

Pathology, the logic of paths

The topography of paths is more than the sum of their parts,
so ponder the motives of those who have preceded you
and be mindful of the interests of those who may follow;
for the logic of paths is a mystery only understood
by those who do not need them.
Remember, each path comes with a purpose
even if it has been long forgotten.
Your rights are leasehold,
your responsibilities surprisingly onerous
so there is no point in arguing the toss about directions.
Registration of paths is a heresy widely misunderstood,
a change to the way of a path contrary to its nature,
to make it straight the height of human folly.
Consider also the unfinished path through the minefield,
or the way to the unmarked grave.

The names of paths

South Vennel, The Cut,
Down-by-the-shore, Badgerbank,
Top Field, The Broomway,
Via Dolorosa, Narachan,
Up-by-Maggie's, Hadrian's Wall,
The Langdyke.

The seductiveness of unmarked paths

A random path is a contradiction
only resolved by discerning its secrets.
In taking the oasis for granted you may forget
that camels often have preferences
which are not the same as yours.
Why, for instance, would you need a path across a frozen lake?
The path taken through Birnam Wood
frequently feels unlike the time before.
A river will find its own path,
a current adapt unerringly to circumstances.
Even a sheep may know its own way.

The mapmaker's urge to destroy signposts

See cairns? Ye dinnae need them.
Signs ur pure rubbish,
way-marks only fit
fir daupet coofs wha couldnae pish themselves.
Gin ye huv a map
jist huv the gumption tae ken yur whauraboots
and gin ye dinna
jist bide at hame in bed.

An amazing way through the labyrinth

The pathway to enlightenment
is a new one on me
needing perseverance and fortitude,
demanding precise answers.
Are we nearly there?
Ask yourself, why are random numbers slippery?
What is the colour of an unsaid prayer?
When is god pretending?
Are we nearly there?

9.30 a.m. Monday, October 11th

The wind is round to the north
degrees colder since last night.
You can feel autumn and just for a minute
before it sinks in a sump of cloud
thin early sun catches the white horses
that are in such a hurry this morning
crowding down the Clyde
like rioters pursued by police.

Everything's leaving, the whole sea sucked south,
so let's go too, wherever they're heading,
catching up everything, taking it with them,
like looters with too much to choose from —
flotsam and guillemots, unwary gulls,
whole boats, boats of every description,
ferries and dinghies, creelers and tankers
and dredgers, even a submarine.

We'll all end up somewhere,
swept out of this place
where autumn is coming,
and not caring a fig
in the sluicing rush of it,
half drowned by the bobbing and rolling,
waving goodbye with mistless eyes
to taste the clean hit of surprise at what's next.

A sense of islands

You can feel them now
after all the long days
and the wastes of dark water

over the gunwales
somewhere out there
beyond the vacancies

we have been skimming surfaces
with nothing to cling to
and no sideways pull of land

minding only the undertow
of our planned destination—
nothing to say

and no interim
save what sucked us forward
to the future we thought we knew.

But tonight there is something
to haunt us. We could jump ship
ride the breakers

be jetsam in a new place
or be reeled in
woozy and sun-dazed.

St Elmo's fire

Still adrift after all these years
but never until now such darkness,
the night thick as sump oil, the tiller slack
in sea that's asphalt-flat;
and no portents,
all stalled by mist that gives air substance,
makes limbo palpable.

And yet, once,
a time lashed to the helm,
the wind turning waves turtle,
spume thrown sideways,
every star banished,
and round the topmost mast among the shrouds
a strange, blithe light, St Elmo's fire.

July

rain again like static on the roof
we live our days in the light
of an aquarium, strange fish,
so many weeks since my blood was warm

the crow immobile on the wire
a heron on the shore, folded
between pitted pewter sea
and unreflecting sky

we came here in our own tight skins
intent on tasting days one at a time
not knowing they run together
like milk spilled across the floor

Boundary

Below the cliffs stand villas, tidy lawns:
raised beach, the man says breezily,
same all along this stretch of coast.

Today the white horses are at a safe distance.
Back then high tide lapped mud-green weed
across where now are kitchen floors.

Living here would set you wondering
how it was then, how it might be again:
that raising, that was more like

a slow falling,
a dropping down of boundaries
so grown-used-to that no one even notices
when what has been there all along finds itself stranded,

out of its depth in air.

Journal: 5th June

Today our way has been unremarkable
until this stream, its bed smoothed from rock
grained with all manner of colours,
pearl and umber and shades of fine linen,
and dry now after all the dry months
save in one last pool where it has poured
and fallen brackish as the fish died;
                              and he,
is clambering down now, spying movement,
his poles and hat and all his equipment
abandoned in the panic of reaching
this shrunken world where, there on his knees,
he fastens round the stifled silver thing
cupped in his hands and drowned in air.

Bothy lands

Peanmeanach, Leacraithnaich,
Strathchailleach, Staoineag, Craig…

Across the firth the Quiraing's jigsaw fret
is topped again by April snows
just as when families arrived
to claim their Homes for Heroes.

All over now: moors marching back
from scoured shingle, lousewort and broomrape
clinging on. For fear of falling masonry
the house is closed with health and safety tape.

Out in the Minch the famished gannets gorge on plastic
line their guts with shreds of carrier bags.
Inland, stacked beach-high behind the tide lines,
cartons, a lube oil drum among the yellow flags.

The bridge has gone—a lone Lands Ender
heading South was almost drowned—
but though the talk's of open access
all futures now are settled on The Mound—

glens bright with plans,
bankers talking dirty down in Edinburgh
of how they'll bring the salmon
back to how they were.

Birders scan the empty shorelines
toting top Swarovski bins.
Sharks sieve thinning seas for plankton,
thresh accusatory fins.

Peanmeanach, Leacraithnaich,
Strathchailleach, Staoineag, Craig…

Beinn Chabhair

Hills ride like icebergs on an earthbound sea.
The ridge up here is dazzle-forested,
light thick as foliage.
Sheared by wind we scale this rock
ours at the zenith of the day
when with a soundless thwunk
a creature tops the cairn and hops
a few considered feet to plant itself
talons splayed against the snow,
as black as snow is white. And wait.

For what? He must have an inkling
for he's tracked our stumbling starts and stops.
The massive anvil of his beak
and gimlet eyes offer no clue
for he takes his cues only from the wind,
fixed not on the famished scrawniness
that aches beneath his gloss of feathers,
but outside on a mind echo
of past instances of awful prodigality,
of littered crusts and cores.

Naked

You must have hopped in
while the door was ajar
bringing with you a pattern
from the spaces between
tall stems and stalks
the dark marsh grass
behind the shed.

Beneath the light I see
through your hopeless camouflage
the mad mosaic of browns
and greens, your landscape;
and when I bend and kneel—
my eye almost the level of yours—
your eye is an unwinking bead.

Among the upright legs of chairs
you pulse a gentler rhythm.
Cupped in my palms
I encompass you.
We are surrounded by upholstery
and household equipment—
the two of us, skin to skin.

Out in the marshy bit behind the shed
from my bare hands you slip
naked into soft rain.
From underneath my hood
I look in vain amongst the grass
for where you've gone
and kneel, and feel the ground.

Skara Brae Buddo

The 5000 year old whalebone figurine is in the Stromness Museum. It was discovered at the Skara Brae archaeological site and has been dubbed 'Buddo' from the Orkney word for friend.

News Report, June 2016

You are naked, as when you were born
from the carver's hand, from the whittle
of stone on bone. You peer through eyes
deep-set, and I have fallen for your spell.
Here on this world's skin
we eye each other up through glass
as thin as five thousand years.

Sleeping beauty, tubby little wench,
how does your awakening feel
after those years beneath the sand?
A morning came when once again
you felt a human warmth
like when my brothers made you
crouched around the fire.

Did it come as a surprise, your second life
as part of human sisterhood?
Peedy sister, bony love,
I think we two are of a kind.
Tell me of your whaley time
before, when you swam the old, cold seas
warmed by whale's blood.

Bone girl

Item found at Dolni Vestonici, Moravia: the oldest known portrait of a woman, sculpted from mammoth ivory c. 26,000 years ago.

This golden bone
was dreamed of and searched for,
found and hoarded.
Back in the cave,
when the thought came
it was chipped and etched
out of eyes reach.

He stole your face,
helped it to find its way out
from where it was hidden.
In the end
he was able to hold you,
to feel your head
between his hands.

*

And what did you think
when you saw what he'd made,
his handiwork:
your face looking back
out of the bone?
Did your eyes meet?
Did you touch one another?

*

Golden bone-girl,
your face drowned now
in warm light and held in space
like a setting on a ring.
An Ice Age away,
we file around you,
see you for one of us.

Snow boys at the Castle Flats

He was as tall as either of us
could reach, his ice-balled head
heaved up and planted
with stones and sticks,
snow-bald save for the bread-bin hat,
arms branched with dead twigs

and, still snagging at my mind,
not the monster-man himself
but all his pint-sized progeny,
the afterthought of orphan snow-boys
untidying the landscape
in their thin, lost crowd—

such a meagre tribe of drifters
strung out across waste ground, a cold
queue of desperate might-have-beens, hardly born,
and never quite reaching the path,
frozen in their flight from the big man,
knowing they'd be the first to melt.

Stopping in snow

Was it like this? Or that?
How do I know?
That night along the railway track—
was there snow?

There had been surely,
though did you wait for me?
And did the signal man invite
us up inside his box and give us tea?

Did he really stop the mail train
to take us home?
Or have these things I think I know
become less known?

Hunched in the guards-van
with all those men on stools
how did it come about
that, contrary to all the rules,

we helped to sort News Chronicles
for people in Manchester?
This much I know:
we stopped, somewhere,

somewhere along the line that night,
in all our winter clothes,
under a moon—was there?—
out in the snow.

Saying their names

Moonless, the night thick,
sky as dark as cloth,
air warm and skin-close, but listen,
chock full of night creatures,
and I am feeling my way along the lane
to find glowworms. Here's one,
then three, four, more...
they shine like distant lanterns,
too low to be stars,
too many to count,
and from the edge of memory
the ghosts return...

playmates and lovers
and brothers-in-arms
who each for a while
meant more than safety or money,
whose names I say
and feel now, a hand held,
a whole minute
of helpless laughter,
a shared silence,
and down the road
each smudge of light
becomes a far-off beacon.

Another life

Another week dropping from sight
like the line of land from the ship's railing

sand and small boats and houses
and then the blur of all that remains
dazed patterns of woodland and headland.

Another life and I would have lingered
shore-bound where the shapes of home
and small things stayed in their proper places

or clambered higher, to draw out the day
moment by moment and take the horizon with me
the sight of the brave boat, sinking to a speck.

Lightning Source UK Ltd.
Milton Keynes UK
UKHW011959300619
345322UK00001B/12/P